SPOTLIGHT ON NATIVE AMERICANS

SHOSHONE

Rodney Kleid

New York

Published in 2016 by The Rosen Publishing Group, Inc.
29 East 21st Street, New York, NY 10010

First Edition

Editor: Karolena Bielecki
Book Design: Kris Everson
Reviewed by: Robert J. Conley, Former Sequoyah Distinguished Professor at Western Carolina University and Director of Native American Studies at Morningside College and Montana State University
Supplemental material reviewed by: Donald A. Grinde, Jr., Professor of Transnational/American Studies at the State University of New York at Buffalo.

Library of Congress Cataloging-in-Publication Data

Kleid, Rodney.
  Shoshone / Rodney Kleid.
    pages cm. — (Spotlight on Native Americans)
  Includes bibliographical references and index.
  ISBN 978-1-4994-1681-7 (pbk.)
  ISBN 978-1-4994-1680-0 (6 pack)
  ISBN 978-1-4994-1683-1 (library binding)
  1. Shoshoni Indians—History—Juvenile literature. 2. Shoshoni Indians—Social life and customs—Juvenile literature. I. Title.
  E99.S4K52 2015
  978.004'974574—dc23
                                                2015007819

CPSIA Compliance Information: Batch #WS15PK: For Further Information contact Rosen Publishing, New York, New York at 1-800-237-9932

CONTENTS

SHOSHONE ORIGINS
CHAPTER 1

The Shoshones inhabit the Great Basin and high plains of the western United States located in today's Nevada, Utah, Idaho, California, Montana, Oregon, and Wyoming. Many Shoshone bands shared a language. The Shoshones called themselves *Nimi*, *Newe*, or *Nomo*, which means "the people." Over time, some bands migrated north and east and changed their lifestyles based on where they lived.

Today, more than 9,250 Shoshones (or Shoshonis) live on **reservations**, **colonies**, and *rancherias* in those states and across the United States.

In Wyoming, the Eastern Shoshones share the Wind River Indian Reservation with the Arapahos. Most Northern Shoshones, who share a **culture** with a people called the Bannocks, live on the Fort Hall Reservation in eastern Idaho. The Western Shoshones live on the Duck Valley Reservation in Nevada and in other communities in Nevada, Utah, and California.

Scientists say that the **ancestors** of the Shoshones may have been from Asia. According to a Shoshone origin story, Wolf formed the earth from a mud ball, and Coyote filled the earth with people. His sons and daughters jumped out of a woven willow water jug Coyote carried across the land, which is why there are so many different Shoshone bands scattered over a large area.

California's Owens Valley, with Mount Whitney in the background, is home to many Western Shoshones, who moved there once their traditional territories could no longer support them.

WESTERN SHOSHONES
CHAPTER 2

Horseless, the Shoshones walked everywhere, using the abundant grasses growing on their lands for shelter and for food, which they produced from the seeds. They also gathered other foods as they found them. Their lifestyle remained largely unchanged until white miners discovered gold at the Comstock Lode in Nevada in 1857. This brought hordes of European-American settlers and miners to the area, pushing out the Native Americans. The Shoshones fought back.

Shoshone raids on the settlers resulted in the 1863 **Treaty** of Ruby Valley, in which the Western Shoshones agreed to leave the settlers alone and live on a reservation in Ruby Valley in today's Nevada. Since the U.S. government did not provide that reservation, the Shoshones continued to live in communities in their traditional areas. In 1877, the government ordered all the Western Shoshones to move to the Duck Valley Reservation created for them on the Idaho-Nevada border. Some moved, but many Shoshones, unhappy with this solution, refused.

Two Shoshones photographed by C.W. Carter in the second half of the nineteenth century, around the time that the Shoshones were forced onto reservations.

As the settlers and their livestock overran Western Shoshone land, they ate or trampled sources of traditional Shoshone foods. Starving Shoshone men began working as cowboys on local ranches for wages, while the women became servants in the ranch houses.

NORTHERN SHOSHONES
CHAPTER 3

With similar cultures, Northern Shoshones and Bannocks lived in small bands in Idaho, south of the Salmon River, in the Columbia River plateau. In 1804, one member of the Lemhi band of Northern Shoshones was the first Northern Shoshone to see white explorers. Her name was Sacagawea, and she traveled with Meriwether Lewis and William Clark on their explorations across the western United States.

On foot until other native tribes traded horses with them in about 1700, the Northern Shoshones combined the Western Shoshone gathering society with the Eastern Shoshone's buffalo-hunting society. Unfortunately, the Blackfeet Indians, who already had horses and guns, began to take over Shoshone territory.

By 1850, settlers moving to Oregon crossed Northern Shoshone country in great numbers, and by 1860, the Mormons, a religious group, had settled in their territory. The Shoshones occasionally battled these intruders, fighting in the Bannock War of 1878 and the Sheepeater War of 1879.

This painting shows the Lewis and Clark expedition with their Shoshone guide Sacagawea and her husband.

EASTERN SHOSHONES
CHAPTER 4

The Eastern Shoshone bands traditionally occupied an area in western Wyoming. Their hunting and gathering lifestyle was strongly affected by the Plains Indian horse culture. A highly organized, buffalo-hunting people, the Eastern Shoshones raided surrounding areas and hunted from horseback after getting horses in about 1700 through trade. From 1780 to 1825, constant warfare with the Blackfeet forced them farther west and reduced their numbers. Some Eastern Shoshones moved south and became known as the Comanches. Smallpox, a deadly disease, spread, killing many Shoshones and further weakening their society.

Chief Washakie rose to power from 1825 to 1880 and restored the spirit and strength of the Eastern Shoshones. Avoiding conflict with the U.S. government, he worked with it on the first Fort Bridger Treaty of July 3, 1863, to establish the Shoshone Reservation, which originally included more than 44 million acres (18 million hectares) in Colorado, Utah, Idaho, and Wyoming. Further agreements and treaties shrunk the

The Eastern Shoshones participated in an annual event during the 1820s through 1840 called the Green River **Rendezvous**. Native Americans, fur trappers, and traders gathered each summer near present-day Pinedale, Wyoming, to trade furs for goods, meet friends, and share news as shown in this 1870s painting. The rendezvous is still held each year during July.

Shoshone Reservation, and in 1878, the U.S. government sent the Shoshones' old enemies, the Arapahos, to share the reservation with them and later renamed it the Wind River Reservation. Today, the Wind River Reservation, home to both the Eastern Shoshones and Arapahos, covers 2,268,000 acres (918,000 ha).

SHRINKING TRIBAL LANDS

CHAPTER 5

The U.S. government made several treaties with the Shoshones during the 1860s, establishing the 1,800,000-acre (730,000-ha) Fort Hall Reservation in 1867 for the Northern Shoshones. The reservation did not remain this size for long, however. Settlers soon illegally moved to reservation land, and the growing town of Pocatello nearby required even more territory. Tribal lands shrank further when the Dawes Severalty Act of 1887 divided them and gave individual pieces to Native American families from 1911 through 1916. The lands were dry; many farms failed and were sold to non-natives, again reducing the tribe's land holdings. By the 1950s, the Fort Hall Reservation covered only 524,000 acres (212,000 ha).

The Shoshones and Bannocks of Fort Hall organized as a tribe with a **constitution** in 1936. In 1963, the Indian Claims Commission awarded $8,864,000 to the Shoshone-Bannocks as a result of a 1946 Indian Claims Commission case against the government for the loss

These Shoshone-Bannock cowboys worked hard to move their cattle swiftly to stay ahead of a prairie fire during the annual roundup at Fort Hall Reservation in 1958.

of their land. Two-thirds of the money was split among the tribal members and one-third given to the tribe as a whole. Since the early twentieth century, their economy has been based on farming, raising sheep and cattle, and **phosphate** mining.

SHARED SHOSHONE CUSTOMS

CHAPTER 6

The Shoshone bands each developed their own unique customs but shared some practices in common.

To protect their skin from the sun, babies were covered with a paste made of clay. They were wrapped in skins and carried in **cradleboards** on their mothers' backs. Young children spent time helping their parents or playing with household items. Older boys played in groups and hunted rabbits, birds, and other small animals, or they helped the older hunters. Older girls helped with household chores and cared for the younger children.

When Shoshone girls became teenagers, they were isolated in a hut for a few days while their mothers spoke with them about proper behavior to prepare them for marriage. No customs existed for a boy's coming of age, except among the Eastern Shoshones, whose boys might go on a **vision quest**.

Marriages were arranged by bride and groom or their families. In some cases, the groom kidnapped the bride and forced her to marry him. Having more than one husband or wife was accepted. Often, a man would have to work for the bride's family before he could marry her. Both marriage and divorce were casual and without ceremony.

WESTERN SHOSHONE TRADITIONS

CHAPTER 7

The Western Shoshones relied upon plant gathering for food. From spring through fall, small family groups wandered over a large area gathering seeds, grasses,

Seeds of the pinion pine tree, pine nuts (also called pinion nuts or seeds) nestle inside a hard shell that must first be removed. The Shoshones ground these nuts to make a fine meal that they added to soups or used like flour in baking.

and plants. In a few weeks, a Shoshone family of four could gather 1,200 pounds (540 kg) of pine nuts, their most important food. They used woven grass baskets to store their seed harvest. The men and boys also hunted rabbits and other small animals.

During winter, many families gathered together at a winter camp. Made from poles, brush, and bark, the Shoshones' winter home was cone-shaped. Women wore hats and skirts of grass, bark, or animal skins, and men wore skin **breechcloths**. Everyone put on rabbit-skin blankets and **moccasins** when it got cold.

Western Shoshones did not have permanent chiefs. When families gathered for a rabbit hunt or festival or in their winter village, the oldest able man was temporarily in charge.

Festivals were for visiting, gambling, and dancing, especially the popular round dance, where many people danced in a circle, accompanied by a singer and drummer. Although the Western Shoshones had few religious ceremonies, men and women spoke directly to the spirits and could acquire a **supernatural** power through dreams and visions.

NORTHERN SHOSHONE TRADITIONS

CHAPTER 8

Although the Northern Shoshones hunted buffalo in large groups like other Plains Indians, fish provided much of their food. Ranging along the Snake River, the Shoshones caught salmon, trout, perch, and other fish. They also collected camas lily and other roots to eat, and hunted elk, deer, and sheep in the mountains.

The Northern Shoshones traded extensively, gaining horses and exchanging furs for other goods. Some Shoshone bands lived in **tepees** like their Plains

The Snake River bends through Grand Teton National Park, Wyoming.

neighbors, while other bands built small, cone-shaped lodges of woven willow branches covered with sage and grass.

The Northern Shoshone bands usually had no chief, unless they were doing something where leadership was necessary, such as gathering for a ceremony, a buffalo hunt, or other community event. Anyone who was brave and a good leader could be a chief; chiefs often changed from event to event.

Their ceremonies were dances held to celebrate the salmon and ask for a good food supply. Like their Eastern Shoshone neighbors, the Northern Shoshones performed the Sun Dance ceremony to bring good to the tribe.

Chief Tendoy of the Lemhi band of Northern Shoshones arranged to have a small reservation set aside for his band in 1875 in the Lemhi Valley, their traditional area. In 1906, the reservation was closed down, and the Shoshones had to move to the Fort Hall Reservation. Chief Tendoy died in 1907.

EASTERN SHOSHONE TRADITIONS

CHAPTER 9

Among the Eastern Shoshones, women created leatherwork. They gained respect by making beautifully decorated parfleches, which were used by the family, given as gifts, and traded for other goods.

Following the available food sources, the Eastern Shoshones roamed across today's Wyoming, settling in different places for months. In addition to buffalo, the men caught fish and hunted deer, sheep, and rabbits. The women gathered roots, seeds, berries, and spring shoots, cared for children, and created leatherwork, especially leather bags called parfleches. They lived in tepees made of tanned buffalo hides.

The Eastern Shoshones believed that all living things had spirits and sought supernatural powers from these spirits through prayers, dreaming, and vision quests. They also held group ceremonies, especially the Sun Dance and the Shuffling Dance, held at night during the winter when they sang **sacred** songs praying for the welfare of the tribe.

The Eastern Shoshones' leader was typically an important older military man respected by the tribe. His leadership determined the strength or weakness of the whole tribe. Because they were involved in the fur trade and were constantly at war with other tribes, good hunters, traders, and warriors were important people in Eastern Shoshone society.

Shoshone women used the type of digging stick shown above (right) to pull up various plants and roots such as the camas lily bulbs. One method of catching fish involved using a woven fish trap, pictured above (left).

Both horses and dogs were necessary to the Shoshones for transportation, hunting, and war. If a horse was wounded in war, it would be painted and decorated with feathers in its mane and tail.

THE SHOSHONE TODAY
CHAPTER 10

Today, Shoshones may live on reservations, colonies, or rancherias, or in numerous American communities. Their lifestyle is similar to that of other Americans, but they still maintain their tribal identities. Some Shoshone children attend reservation schools; others go to local public schools. Since the 1960s, many Shoshone communities have renewed their tradition of annual festivals.

Begun in the 1990s, the Shoshone Tribal Cultural Center on the Wind River Reservation provides tribal history and teaching of the Shoshone language and traditional arts and crafts. Religion is still very important, and many Eastern Shoshones participate in the Sun Dance and in the Native American Church, which combines Native beliefs and customs with Christianity. **Powwows** were introduced in 1957 and have become important social and cultural events. In the 1970s, Shoshone women began to sing, drum, and perform some dances traditionally done by men.

Modern powwows feature food, traditional arts, and popular dance competitions. Here, a Shoshone girl performs a shawl dance.

While many Shoshones participate in the powwows, Western Shoshones call their festival a "fandango." Traditionally lasting a week, Shoshone bands renewed friendships, made new friends, and hunted together. Dancing, food, and prayers have long been part of a fandango. Now, the festival lasts Friday through Sunday and includes a barbecue, games, traditional songs and dances, and arts and crafts.

THE SHOSHONE ECONOMY

CHAPTER 11

The Shoshone land base continues to change. In 2000, the Timbisha Shoshones, part of the Western Shoshones, began a new reservation in Death Valley, California. Since there are no jobs or housing there, no one lives on the Northwestern Shoshone band's 184 acres (75 ha) in Utah.

The Indian Relay races have been a tradition at Fort Hall Reservation for over one hundred years.

Government improvement programs rarely help those not living on large reservations.

The Northern Shoshones on the Fort Hall Reservation established their first **casino** in 1990. Today, the Fort Hall Reservation's casinos attract over 200,000 tourists a year. The Fort Hall Reservation also promotes education in both English and Shoshone, publishes a local newspaper called the *Sho-Ban News*, and holds yearly festivals.

After their casino opened in 1990, the Northern Shoshones were involved in legal battles with the Idaho government, which did not want any casinos within the state. Finally in 2000, a law passed allowing the tribe to have casinos.

The money gained from leasing the right to big businesses to drill for oil and gas on their land contributes to the tribal economy of the Eastern Shoshones, as does ranching and farming. The unemployment rate is still high, however, and young people leave the reservation for better education and employment opportunities.

SHOSHONE ARTS
CHAPTER 12

Many Shoshones contribute to American arts and literature, bringing their own unique ideas. Based upon the traditional craft of weaving baskets to store seed harvests, Shoshone grass basketry thrives as an art form today. Painting pictures on animal hides was once popular but has now almost died

Recognized as works of art today, Shoshone woven grass baskets were used to store seed harvests.

out. Shoshone beadwork is still produced and is very popular at powwows. The beadwork designs were originally abstract, but in the twentieth century, plant and animal designs became popular. Today many of the most skilled Shoshone designs feature realistic images of flowers.

Sandra Okuma, who is Shoshone-Bannock and Luiseno, paints pictures of Native Americans that focus on the detail and beauty of traditional or powwow clothing. Her daughter, Jamie, creates soft sculptures with elaborate beadwork. Both mother

These Shoshone beaded moccasins were created around a hundred years ago on the Wind River Reservation in Wyoming.

and daughter have won awards in recognition of their skills.

A former teacher, carpenter, and cowboy, Western Shoshone Jack Malotte is a well-known graphic artist. He loves painting landscapes but is most famous for his humorous and political paintings. His pictures show what it's like to be a traditional Indian in a modern American world. The Smithsonian's National Museum of the American Indian featured his work in its "Indian Humor" exhibition.

ISSUES FACING THE SHOSHONE

CHAPTER 13

In 1948, the U.S. government started using the Nevada Test Site in Western Shoshone territory to test nuclear bombs. The Shoshones and others who object to the use of nuclear weapons and nuclear energy hold protests around the site and at nearby Yucca Mountain. They also hold **vigils** for lives lost due to **radiation** from nuclear testing.

A major issue faced by the Shoshones is the loss of Western Shoshone land to American settlers. The Indian Claims Commission approved of paying back the Shoshones in 1979. These funds were never given to the tribe. Some Western Shoshones were afraid that if they accepted the money, they would never get their land back.

In 2003, the U.S. Senate also approved paying the Western Shoshones $142 million. The Western Shoshone National Council and others went to court in 2003, however, to ask for the return of 60 million acres (24 million ha) in four states, land that they call Newe

These Northern Shoshone girls have fun together at a local celebration. Pride in their heritage will help keep the Shoshone tribe strong.

Sogobia. The non-profit Western Shoshone Defense Project continues to fight for the Western Shoshone today.

Today's Shoshones face **poverty** and unemployment. They fight to maintain their traditional lands, keep their sacred places untouched, and educate people about their special history and culture. Keeping their traditional communities alive ensures the Shoshone people will overcome their struggles and preserve their culture.

GLOSSARY

ancestor: Someone in your family who lived long before you.

breechcloth: A strip of cloth worn around the hips.

casino: A building where gambling takes place.

colony: A piece of land under the control of another country.

constitution: The basic laws and principles of a nation that outline the powers of the government and the rights of the people.

cradleboard: Portable cradle made of a board or frame onto which a baby is secured with blankets or binding.

culture: The arts, beliefs, and customs that form a people's way of life.

moccasins: Soft shoes made of a single piece of leather.

phosphate: A salt or compound that's used in fertilizers and strong cleaners.

poverty: The state of being poor.

powwow: A social gathering of Native Americans that usually includes dancing.

radiation: Waves of energy, which are sometimes harmful to people and animals.

rancheria: Small reservation given to Native Americans in California.

rendezvous: A meeting set for a specific time and place.

reservation: Land set aside by the government for specific Native American tribes to live on.

sacred: Specially blessed.

supernatural: Unable to be explained by science or the laws of nature.

tepee: A tent that is shaped like a cone and was used in the past by some Native Americans as a house.

treaty: An agreement among nations or people.

vigil: An event at which people stay awake through the night to support a cause or pray.

vision quest: A journey into the wilderness taken by a Native American teenage boy to seek spiritual power from the supernatural world.

FOR MORE INFORMATION

BOOKS

Norwich, Grace. *I Am Sacagawea*. New York, NY:
Scholastic, 2012.

Rajczak, Kristen. *The Shoshone People*. New York, NY:
Gareth Stevens, 2015.

Sonneborn, Liz. *The Shoshones*. Minneapolis, MN: Lerner
Publications, 2007.

WEBSITES

Due to the changing nature of Internet links, PowerKids Press has
developed an online list of websites related to the subject of this book.
This site is updated regularly. Please use this link to access the list:
www.powerkidslinks.com/sona/sho

INDEX